8 Secrets To
REDISCOVERING
Joy And Purpose
On Your **JOURNEY**

TOMORROW'S RESILIENT WOMAN

JOURNAL

DR. LAKRISHIA COOK

Table of Contents

Table of Contents

INTRODUCTION

A Journey of Grace, Resilience, and Rediscovery

Healing is not a race—it's a sacred process. It unfolds in layers, revealing strength in spaces we once saw only brokenness. If you're holding this journal in your hands, it's because something within you is seeking restoration, clarity, and the courage to move forward. And I want you to know—you are exactly where you need to be.

This journal is more than just pages with prompts. It's a **tool, a companion, a safe space** to process, reflect, and deepen your healing journey. It was designed to walk alongside the wisdom of the book you're reading, providing **structured moments of reflection, intentional prayers, and scripture-based encouragement** that will guide you toward rediscovery and renewal.

But here's the thing—there is no rush. Healing is deeply personal, and **you are allowed to take your time.** I encourage you to move through these pages **slowly, intentionally, and without pressure**. There is no right or wrong way to engage with this journal. Some days, the words might flow effortlessly. Other days, you may sit in silence, simply allowing the scriptures and affirmations to settle within you.

Let yourself feel. Let yourself pause. Let yourself lean into grace.

You are not alone on this journey. And as you explore these prompts and scriptures, I pray that each word reminds you of **your resilience, your purpose, and the unwavering love that surrounds you**.

Anchor Yourself in Grace

Theme: Finding Stability in God's Love and Presence

Weekly Focus:

Grace is the foundation that holds us steady when life feels uncertain. This week, we explore how to embrace God's grace, trust in His promises, and allow His love to anchor our hearts.

DAY

1

The Gift of Grace

Scripture: Ephesians 2:8 – "For it is by grace you have been saved, through faith—and this is not from yourselves, it is the gift of God."

Journaling Prompt: Describe a time when you felt completely unworthy but experienced grace anyway. How did it change your perspective?

_____

_____

_____

_____

_____

_____

_____

_____

Affirmation: "I am held by God's grace, not by my mistakes."

DAY

2

Receiving Grace When You Feel Undeserving

Scripture: Romans 8:1 – "Therefore, there is now no condemnation for those who are in Christ Jesus."

Journaling Prompt: What negative thoughts or guilt do you need to surrender today? Write them out, then release them in prayer.

_____

_____

_____

_____

_____

_____

_____

_____

Affirmation: "I am forgiven, I am loved, I am free."

DAY

3

Anchoring Yourself in God's Presence

Scripture: Psalm 46:1 – "God is our refuge and strength, an ever-present help in trouble."

Journaling Prompt: Where do you feel closest to God? How can you make space for His presence in your daily routine?

_____

_____

_____

_____

_____

_____

_____

_____

Affirmation: "God is my safe place—I will rest in His presence."

4

Shifting from Self-Sufficiency to Trust

Scripture: Proverbs 3:5-6 – "Trust in the Lord with all your heart and lean not on your own understanding."

Journaling Prompt: What areas of your life are you trying to control? How can you practice surrendering them to God?

_____

_____

_____

_____

_____

_____

_____

_____

Affirmation: "I release control and trust in God's plan."

DAY

5

Grace and Healing

Scripture: Psalm 147:3 – "He heals the brokenhearted and binds up their wounds."

Journaling Prompt: What wounds are you carrying? How does knowing God is your healer bring you comfort?

_____

_____

_____

_____

_____

_____

_____

_____

_____

Affirmation: "My pain does not define me—God is making me whole."

DAY

6

Cultivating a Grace-Filled Mindset

Scripture: Philippians 4:8 – "Whatever is true, whatever is noble, whatever is right... think about such things."

Journaling Prompt: Write down three negative thoughts that often cross your mind. Now, rewrite them as grace-filled truths.

_____

_____

_____

_____

_____

_____

_____

_____

Affirmation: "I choose to see myself the way God sees me—worthy and loved."

DAY

7

Living in Grace Daily

Scripture: 2 Corinthians 12:9 – "My grace is sufficient for you, for my power is made perfect in weakness."

Journaling Prompt: How can you extend grace to yourself and others today? Write a prayer asking for God's help.

_____

_____

_____

_____

_____

_____

_____

_____

Affirmation: "Grace is my daily strength—I will walk in it fully."

Release the Weight of the Past

Theme: Letting Go, Forgiveness, and Emotional Freedom

Weekly Focus:

Releasing the weight of the past frees you to step into joy and healing. This week, we focus on forgiveness, emotional release, and the power of surrender.

1

Recognizing What's Holding You Back

Scripture: Hebrews 12:1 – "Let us throw off everything that hinders and the sin that so easily entangles."

Journaling Prompt: What emotions, grudges, or regrets weigh you down? Make a list and reflect on their impact.

_____

_____

_____

_____

_____

_____

_____

Affirmation: "I am ready to release what no longer serves me."

DAY
2

The Power of Forgiveness

Scripture: Colossians 3:13 – "Forgive as the Lord forgave you."

Journaling Prompt: Who or what do you need to forgive? Write a letter expressing your thoughts (even if you never send it).

_____

_____

_____

_____

_____

_____

_____

_____

_____

Affirmation: "Forgiveness sets me free—I choose to walk in freedom."

DAY

3

Releasing Self-Blame

Scripture: Isaiah 43:18-19 – "Forget the former things; do not dwell on the past. See, I am doing a new thing!"

Journaling Prompt: Are you holding yourself hostage to past mistakes? Write down what you need to release today.

_____

_____

_____

_____

_____

_____

_____

_____

Affirmation: "I am worthy of a fresh start."

DAY

4

Releasing Hurt Through Prayer

Scripture: Matthew 11:28 – "Come to me, all you who are weary and burdened, and I will give you rest."

Journaling Prompt: Write a prayer asking God to help you release emotional burdens. Speak it aloud with faith.

_____

_____

_____

_____

_____

_____

_____

_____

Affirmation: "I release my pain and step into peace."

5

Breaking Free from Limiting Beliefs

Scripture: Romans 12:2 – "Do not conform to the pattern of this world but be transformed by the renewing of your mind."

Journaling Prompt: What lies have you believed about yourself? How can you replace them with God's truth?

_____

_____

_____

_____

_____

_____

_____

_____

Affirmation: "I am not defined by my past—I am transformed by truth."

DAY

6

Releasing Control and Trusting the Process

Scripture: Psalm 55:22 – "Cast your cares on the Lord and He will sustain you."

Journaling Prompt: What fears are keeping you stuck? Write them out and imagine handing them over to God.

_____

_____

_____

_____

_____

_____

_____

_____

Affirmation: "I trust the unfolding of my journey."

DAY

7

Walking in Freedom

Scripture: John 8:36 – "So if the Son sets you free, you will be free indeed."

Journaling Prompt: How do you want to feel moving forward? Write a declaration of freedom for yourself.

_____

_____

_____

_____

_____

_____

_____

_____

Affirmation: "I am free to step into my new beginning."

WEEK 3

Embracing Your Authentic Self

Theme: Self-Discovery, Confidence, and Embracing Who God Created You to Be

Weekly Focus:

God designed you with purpose, beauty, and uniqueness—yet too often, we shrink ourselves to fit expectations that were never meant for us. This week is about rediscovering your authentic self, breaking free from comparison, and stepping into your divinely designed identity with boldness.

DAY

1

Who Does God Say You Are?

Scripture: Jeremiah 1:5 – "Before I formed you in the womb, I knew you; before you were born, I set you apart."

Journaling Prompt: What identities have others placed on you that don't align with who God says you are? Write a declaration of truth about yourself.

_____

_____

_____

_____

_____

_____

_____

Affirmation: "I am chosen, called, and created for a purpose."

DAY

2

Releasing the Fear of Judgment

Scripture: Galatians 1:10 – "Am I now trying to win the approval of human beings, or of God?"

Journaling Prompt: What fears hold you back from fully expressing who you are? How can you release them and step into your authenticity?

_____

_____

_____

_____

_____

_____

_____

_____

Affirmation: "I will not shrink—I am fearfully and wonderfully made."

DAY

3

Breaking Free from Comparison

Scripture: 2 Corinthians 10:12 – "They measure themselves by themselves... but they are not wise."

Journaling Prompt: Where in your life do you compare yourself to others? Write about how that has impacted your self-view and confidence.

_____

_____

_____

_____

_____

_____

_____

Affirmation: "My journey is uniquely mine, and I embrace it fully."

DAY

4

Owning Your Story

Scripture: Romans 8:28 – "God works all things together for good for those who love Him."

Journaling Prompt: Reflect on a painful moment from your past. How has it shaped you into the person you are today?

_____

_____

_____

_____

_____

_____

_____

_____

Affirmation: "My past is part of my testimony, not my identity."

DAY

5

Embracing Your Strengths

Scripture: 1 Peter 4:10 – "Each of you should use whatever gift you have received to serve others."

Journaling Prompt: What are three unique strengths or talents that God has given you? How can you use them more intentionally?

_____

_____

_____

_____

_____

_____

_____

_____

Affirmation: "I honor and embrace my God-given gifts."

DAY

6

Speaking Life Over Yourself

Scripture: Proverbs 18:21 – "The tongue has the power of life and death."

Journaling Prompt: Write down negative things you've spoken over yourself. Now, rewrite them as life-giving affirmations rooted in God's truth.

_____

_____

_____

_____

_____

_____

_____

_____

Affirmation: "I speak truth and grace over my life."

DAY

7

Walking in Confidence

Scripture: 2 Timothy 1:7 – "For God has not given us a spirit of fear, but of power, love, and a sound mind."

Journaling Prompt: How will you walk forward confidently in who God made you to be? Write a personal mission statement.

_____

_____

_____

_____

_____

_____

_____

_____

Affirmation: "I step into my future boldly, trusting that I am enough."

Walking in Purpose

Theme: Living with Intentionality, Discovering Your Calling, and Flourishing in Purpose

Weekly Focus:

Purpose isn't something you chase—it's something you uncover. This week, we explore how to align your life with your divine calling, trust God's timing, and live with intentionality and fulfillment.

DAY

1

Understanding Purpose vs. Passion

Scripture: Proverbs 19:21 – "Many are the plans in a person's heart, but it is the Lord's purpose that prevails."

Journaling Prompt: What excites you? What burdens your heart? How do these connect to the purpose God may be shaping for you?

_____

_____

_____

_____

_____

_____

_____

_____

Affirmation: "I am uniquely designed to live in purpose."

DAY

2

Letting Go of Distractions

Scripture: Hebrews 12:1 – "Let us throw off everything that hinders and run with perseverance the race marked out for us."

Journaling Prompt: What distractions keep you from focusing on your calling? How can you shift your priorities?

_____

_____

_____

_____

_____

_____

_____

_____

Affirmation: "I choose clarity over distractions and focus on God's vision."

3

Trusting God's Timing

Scripture: Ecclesiastes 3:1 – "There is a time for everything, and a season for every activity under the heavens."

Journaling Prompt: What areas of your life require more patience? How can you trust God's timing in those spaces?

_____

_____

_____

_____

_____

_____

_____

_____

Affirmation: "I trust that God's plan for me is unfolding exactly as it should."

DAY

4

Serving Through Your Purpose

Scripture: Matthew 5:16 – "Let your light shine before others, that they may see your good deeds and glorify your Father in heaven."

Journaling Prompt: How can you use your gifts to serve others? Write down three ways to make an impact this week.

_____

_____

_____

_____

_____

_____

_____

_____

_____

Affirmation: "I live with intention, serving in my purpose daily."

5

Overcoming Doubt in Your Calling

Scripture: Exodus 4:12 – "Now go; I will help you speak and teach you what to say."

Journaling Prompt: Where do you struggle with doubt about your purpose? How can you replace those doubts with faith?

_____

_____

_____

_____

_____

_____

_____

_____

Affirmation: "I am equipped and called—I will not let doubt define me."

DAY
6

Aligning Your Life with Purpose

Scripture: Colossians 3:23 – "Whatever you do, work at it with all your heart, as working for the Lord."

Journaling Prompt: How can you shift your daily habits to reflect a life of greater purpose?

_____

_____

_____

_____

_____

_____

_____

_____

Affirmation: "Every action I take moves me closer to my God-given calling."

7

Flourishing Forward in Purpose

Scripture: Philippians 1:6 – "He who began a good work in you will carry it on to completion."

Journaling Prompt: Write a prayer of gratitude for the calling God has placed on your life.

_____

_____

_____

_____

_____

_____

_____

_____

Affirmation: "I am walking boldly into my future, trusting in His plan."

Cultivating Joy in Everyday Life

Theme: Choosing Joy, Practicing Gratitude, and Finding Peace in the Present Moment

Weekly Focus:

Joy isn't found in perfect circumstances—it's cultivated. This week focuses on shifting perspective, practicing gratitude, and embracing joy in both the highs and lows of life.

DAY

1

Redefining Joy

Scripture: Nehemiah 8:10 – "The joy of the Lord is your strength."

Journaling Prompt: What does joy mean to you? How is it different from happiness?

_____

_____

_____

_____

_____

_____

_____

_____

Affirmation: "I choose joy—it is my strength, not my circumstance."

DAY

2

Finding Joy in the Small Moments

Scripture: Psalm 118:24 – "This is the day the Lord has made; let us rejoice and be glad in it."

Journaling Prompt: What small, simple things brought you joy today? How can you become more aware of them?

_____

_____

_____

_____

_____

_____

_____

_____

Affirmation: "Joy is everywhere—I open my heart to notice it."

DAY

3

Releasing Worry to Embrace Peace

Scripture: Philippians 4:6-7 – "Do not be anxious about anything... and the peace of God will guard your hearts."

Journaling Prompt: What worries are stealing your joy? Write them down, then pray about releasing them.

_____

_____

_____

_____

_____

_____

_____

_____

Affirmation: "I surrender my worries and embrace peace."

DAY

4

Choosing Gratitude

Scripture: 1 Thessalonians 5:16-18 – "Rejoice always, pray continually, give thanks in all circumstances."

Journaling Prompt: List five things you're grateful for today. How does gratitude shift your perspective?

_____

_____

_____

_____

_____

_____

_____

_____

Affirmation: "Gratitude fills my heart—I am thankful for every blessing."

5

Finding Joy in Hard Seasons

Scripture: James 1:2-3 – "Consider it pure joy whenever you face trials... because perseverance produces character."

Journaling Prompt: How can challenges lead to growth? Reflect on a past struggle that shaped you positively.

_____

_____

_____

_____

_____

_____

_____

_____

_____

Affirmation: "Even in trials, I trust that joy is waiting for me."

DAY

6

Spreading Joy to Others

Scripture: Proverbs 11:25 – "A generous person will prosper; whoever refreshes others will be refreshed."

Journaling Prompt: How can you bring joy to someone today? Write about ways to uplift others.

_____

_____

_____

_____

_____

_____

_____

_____

Affirmation: "Sharing joy multiplies it—I will be a light to others."

DAY
7
Living Joyfully Daily

Scripture: John 15:11 – "I have told you this so that my joy may be in you and that your joy may be complete."

Journaling Prompt: What habits can you create to sustain joy long-term? Write a personal joy commitment.

_____

_____

_____

_____

_____

_____

_____

_____

Affirmation: "Joy is a daily choice—I will embrace it fully."

WEEK 6

Building Meaningful Connections

Theme: Strengthening Relationships and Creating Community

Weekly Focus:

We are wired for connection, yet relationships can be complicated, requiring vulnerability, intentionality, and trust. This week, we focus on fostering healthy connections, setting boundaries, and finding God-centered community that nourishes your soul.

1

The Purpose of Connection

Scripture: Ecclesiastes 4:9-10 – "Two are better than one... If either of them falls down, one can help the other up."

Journaling Prompt: What relationships have shaped you most in life? Reflect on the impact they've had.

_____

_____

_____

_____

_____

_____

_____

_____

Affirmation: "I am created for meaningful connection and community."

DAY

2

Strengthening Existing Relationships

Scripture: Proverbs 27:17 – "As iron sharpens iron, so one person sharpens another."

Journaling Prompt: Who are the people in your life that uplift and encourage you? How can you invest more in those relationships?

_____

_____

_____

_____

_____

_____

_____

_____

Affirmation: "I cultivate relationships that strengthen and inspire me."

DAY

3

Creating New Connections

Scripture: Hebrews 10:24-25 – "Let us consider how we may spur one another on toward love and good deeds."

Journaling Prompt: What kind of connections are missing in your life right now? Write about ways to find new community.

_____

_____

_____

_____

_____

_____

_____

_____

Affirmation: "I am open to building new, life-giving relationships."

DAY

4

Setting Healthy Boundaries

Scripture: Proverbs 4:23 – "Above all else, guard your heart, for everything you do flows from it."

Journaling Prompt: What boundaries do you need in your relationships? Write about where you struggle with saying no and what you need to change.

_____

_____

_____

_____

_____

_____

_____

_____

Affirmation: "I honor my needs and set boundaries with grace."

DAY

5

Relationships and Forgiveness

Scripture: Ephesians 4:32 – "Be kind and compassionate... forgiving each other, just as Christ forgave you."

Journaling Prompt: Is there someone you need to forgive? How does holding onto resentment affect your ability to connect?

_____

_____

_____

_____

_____

_____

_____

_____

_____

Affirmation: "I choose to walk in forgiveness, releasing the past."

DAY

6

Finding God-Centered Community

Scripture: Acts 2:42 – "They devoted themselves to the apostles' teaching and to fellowship."

Journaling Prompt: What does being part of a community of faith mean to you? How can you be more intentional in seeking out God-centered friendships?

_____

_____

_____

_____

_____

_____

_____

_____

_____

_____

Affirmation: "I surround myself with faith-filled community."

DAY

7

Celebrating Relationships

Scripture: 1 Thessalonians 5:11 – "Encourage one another and build each other up."

Journaling Prompt: Who in your life has been a blessing to you? Write a letter or message of gratitude to them.

_____

_____

_____

_____

_____

_____

_____

_____

_____

Affirmation: "I am grateful for the relationships that bring joy and purpose to my life."

✦✦✦✦✦✦ ✧ ✦✦✦✦✦✦

Overcome Challenges with Resilience

Theme: Strength in Trials and Trusting the Process

Weekly Focus:

Resilience is about rising, not avoiding hardship. This week, we explore how to navigate obstacles with faith, embrace difficult seasons with strength, and lean on God's promises for perseverance.

DAY

1

What Resilience Looks Like

Scripture: James 1:2-3 – "Consider it pure joy... when you face trials, because you know the testing of your faith produces perseverance."

Journaling Prompt: Think about a time you overcame something difficult. What helped you push through?

_____

_____

_____

_____

_____

_____

_____

_____

Affirmation: "I am stronger than my struggles—I rise in resilience."

DAY
2

Leaning into Faith During Hardship

Scripture: Isaiah 41:10 – "Do not fear... I will strengthen and help you."

Journaling Prompt: When life feels overwhelming, where do you turn? How can you deepen your reliance on God's strength?

_____

_____

_____

_____

_____

_____

_____

_____

_____

_____

Affirmation: "I trust that God is my refuge in every storm."

DAY

3

Using Therapeutic Tools for Resilience

Scripture: Psalm 94:19 – "When anxiety was great within me, Your consolation brought joy to my soul."

Journaling Prompt: What coping strategies—faith-based or therapy-inspired—help you process challenges?

_____

_____

_____

_____

_____

_____

_____

_____

Affirmation: "I equip myself with tools that strengthen my mind and spirit."

DAY

4

Shifting Perspective in Difficult Seasons

Scripture: Romans 8:28 – "God works all things together for good for those who love Him."

Journaling Prompt: What difficult situation are you currently facing? What lessons might God be revealing through it?

_____

_____

_____

_____

_____

_____

_____

_____

_____

Affirmation: "Even in struggle, God is working for my good."

DAY

5

Leaning on Support Systems

Scripture: Galatians 6:2 – "Carry each other's burdens, and in this way, you fulfill the law of Christ."

Journaling Prompt: Who in your life helps you through tough times? How can you allow yourself to lean on others more?

_____

_____

_____

_____

_____

_____

_____

_____

Affirmation: "I do not have to walk this journey alone—I am supported."

DAY

6

Strength in Surrender

Scripture: 2 Corinthians 12:9 – "My grace is sufficient for you, for my power is made perfect in weakness."

Journaling Prompt: What are you holding onto that feels too heavy? What would surrendering it to God look like?

_____

_____

_____

_____

_____

_____

_____

_____

Affirmation: "I surrender my worries and receive God's peace."

DAY

7

Walking Forward in Resilience

Scripture: Philippians 3:13-14 – "Forgetting what is behind and straining toward what is ahead... I press on."

Journaling Prompt: How do you want to embody resilience moving forward? Write your personal declaration of strength.

_____

_____

_____

_____

_____

_____

_____

_____

Affirmation: "I am stepping into my future with faith and courage."

Flourishing Forward with Hope

Theme: Stepping into the Future, Trusting God's Plan, and Walking Boldly in Faith

Weekly Focus:

Hope is the fuel that moves us forward. This week is about trusting the unfolding of your journey, embracing the unknown, and stepping confidently into your future with faith.

DAY

1

Hope for What's Ahead

Scripture: Jeremiah 29:11 – "For I know the plans I have for you, declares the Lord, plans to give you hope and a future."

Journaling Prompt: What dreams are stirring in your heart? Write them down, no matter how big they seem.

_____

_____

_____

_____

_____

_____

_____

_____

Affirmation: "I trust that God's plan for me is full of hope."

DAY
2
Overcoming Fear of the Future

Scripture: Isaiah 41:10 – "Do not fear, for I am with you."

Journaling Prompt: What fears do you have about stepping into new seasons? How can faith replace those fears?

_____

_____

_____

_____

_____

_____

_____

_____

_____

Affirmation: "Fear does not define me—I step forward boldly."

3

Letting Go of the Need to Control

Scripture: Proverbs 16:9 – "In their hearts humans plan their course, but the Lord establishes their steps."

Journaling Prompt: Where are you trying to control outcomes? How can you trust God more?

_____

_____

_____

_____

_____

_____

_____

_____

_____

Affirmation: "I release control and trust God's perfect timing."

DAY

4

Preparing for the Next Chapter

Scripture: Psalm 32:8 – "I will instruct you and teach you in the way you should go."

Journaling Prompt: What steps can you take today to move forward in faith?

_____

_____

_____

_____

_____

_____

_____

_____

Affirmation: "I step into new beginnings with confidence."

DAY

5

Walking in Faith, Not Fear

Scripture: 2 Corinthians 5:7 – "For we walk by faith, not by sight."

Journaling Prompt: When have you taken a leap of faith before? What did it teach you?

_____

_____

_____

_____

_____

_____

_____

_____

_____

Affirmation: "I trust God's guidance—I walk by faith."

DAY

6

Seeing Yourself as God Sees You

Scripture: 1 Peter 2:9 – "You are a chosen people, a royal priesthood, a holy nation, God's special possession."

Journaling Prompt: How would your life change if you fully embraced your worth? Write a love letter to yourself.

_____

_____

_____

_____

_____

_____

_____

_____

Affirmation: "I am chosen, called, and deeply loved."

7

Stepping into Your Future
with Confidence

Scripture: Philippians 3:13-14 – "Forgetting what is behind and straining toward what is ahead... I press on."

Journaling Prompt: Write a final reflection on how far you've come during this journal journey.

_____

_____

_____

_____

_____

_____

_____

_____

Affirmation: "I step forward with faith, knowing my future is bright."

CONCLUSION

Stepping Forward with Strength and Hope

As you close the final pages of this journal, take a deep breath. Reflect on how far you've come. Consider the moments when you allowed yourself to **release, rebuild, and rediscover the fullness of who you are**.

This journey wasn't meant to be perfect—it was meant to be **transformative**. You did not have to have all the answers. You simply had to show up, day by day, willing to grow, to heal, and to step forward in faith. And you did.

Your healing does not end here—because healing is an **ongoing process**, not a destination. But now, you step forward **equipped**. You step forward **aware of your strength**. You step forward **knowing that grace will meet you every step of the way**.

So, wherever you go from here, **walk boldly in joy, in resilience, and in the truth that you are deeply loved.**

Thank you for allowing this journal to be a part of your journey. You are ready—more ready than you know.

About the Author

Dr. LaKrishia Cook is a DNP-prepared nurse, author, and mentor dedicated to guiding others through healing, rediscovery, and transformation. With over 25 years of experience in the nursing profession, she understands both the physical and spiritual aspects of healing, inspiring others to embrace resilience and faith.

Her journey has been shaped by deep love and profound loss, including the passing of both parents, the heartbreaking death of her son, infidelity, and a subsequent divorce. These experiences have given her an intimate understanding of grief, allowing her to speak life into those navigating seasons of pain and renewal.

Today, she is a devoted wife to De'Angelo, who reflects Christ's love in her life, and a proud mother to her daughter, Karys, her greatest blessing. She also shares her home with two beloved dogs, Bella and Appa, who bring warmth and companionship to her family.

Through her books, devotionals, and faith-driven coaching, she empowers women to reclaim joy, trust their journey, and embrace God's plan for their lives. This journal is a tool to support, uplift, and help you step boldly into your next season, knowing that healing is possible, and hope is always within reach.

www.ingramcontent.com/pod-product-compliance
Lightning Source LLC
Chambersburg PA
CBHW011218120626
46545CB00008B/3045